# Stourbridge, Wollaston, Amblecote & District

## A SECOND SELECTION

### BOB CLARKE & MICHAEL REUTER

SUTTON PUBLISHING LIMITED

Sutton Publishing Limited
Phoenix Mill · Thrupp · Stroud
Gloucestershire · GL5 2BU

First published 2000

Copyright © Bob Clarke & Michael Reuter,
2000

*Title page photograph*: Lower High Street, late
1800s.

**British Library Cataloguing in Publication Data**
A catalogue record for this book is available from the
British Library.

ISBN 0-7509-2496-9

Typeset in 10.5/13.5 Photina.
Typesetting and origination by
Sutton Publishing Limited.
Printed and bound in England by
J.H. Haynes & Co. Ltd, Sparkford.

## THE BLACK COUNTRY SOCIETY

This voluntary society, affiliated to the Civic Trust, was founded in 1967 as a reaction to the trend of the late 1950s and early 1960s to amalgamate everything into large units and in the Midlands to sweep away the area's industrial heritage in the process.

The general aim of the Society is to create interest in the past, present and future of the Black Country, and early on it campaigned for the establishment of an industrial museum. In 1975 the Black Country Living Museum was started by Dudley Borough Council on 26 acres of totally derelict land adjoining the grounds of Dudley Castle. This has developed into an award-winning museum which attracts over 250,000 visitors annually.

It was announced in August 1998 that having secured a lottery grant of nearly £3 million, the Museum Board will be able to authorize the start of work on a £4.5 million state-of-the-art interpretation centre. This will be known as the 'Rolfe Street Project', named after the street which once housed the Smethwick Baths. The façade of this Victorian building is to be incorporated into the new interpretation centre.

At the Black Country Living Museum there is a boat dock fully equipped to restore narrowboats of wood and iron and different vessels can be seen on the dock throughout the year. From behind the Bottle and Glass Inn visitors can travel on a canal boat into Dudley Canal Tunnel, a memorable journey to see spectacular limestone caverns and the fascinating Castle Mill Basin.

There are 2,500 members of the Black Country Society and all receive the quarterly magazine *The Blackcountryman*, of which 124 issues have been published since its founding in 1967. In the whole collection there are some 1,800 authoritative articles on all aspects of the Black Country by historians, teachers, researchers, students, subject experts and ordinary folk with an extraordinary story to tell. The whole constitutes a unique resource about the area and is a mine of information for students and researchers who frequently refer to it. Many schools and libraries are subscribers. Three thousand copies of the magazine are printed each quarter. It is non-commercial, and contributors do not receive payment for their articles.

*PO Box 71 · Kingswinford · West Midlands DY6 9YN*

# CONTENTS

There's something of a mystery as to who this trader was. The Rye Market shop premises was selling clothing, some, so a sign says, 'at less than cost price'. The puzzling feature is the number of posters referring to the 'selling out' of a fish shop. Above the shop is a business sign where a P. Chance offered his services as a 'letter cutter, engraver, trade mark engraver.' This photograph is thought to date from about 1870.

# INTRODUCTION

lthough Stourbridge, unlike Amblecote, Pedmore and Oldswinford, did not warrant a mention in the Domesday Book – and from that it can be assumed either it didn't exist or was considered worthless – less than two hundred years later it was mentioned in the 1255 Worcester Assize Roll, when its spelling varied between Sturbrug or Sturesbrige.

But what were eventually to become suburbs of Stourbridge – Amblecote (Elmecote), Pedmore (Pavemore) and Oldswinford (Suineford) are specifically mentioned in the Domesday Book. Indeed 'Swinford' is mentioned in a 950 AD Saxon Charter. All three areas were owned by a powerful Norman Lord, William Fitz Ansculf, who governed vast land holdings in the West Midlands from Dudley Castle. At that time the major settlement locally was Swinford with the word 'old' added to differentiate from neighbouring Kingswinford.

Being on the edge of the productive Worcestershire and South Staffordshire countryside, where there was a substantial sheep farming industry, Oldswinford expanded to create what eventually became Stourbridge. By the sixteenth century Stourbridge had become an important market town, a position it was to hold until quite recent times, serving a wide rural area to the west and south.

In the seventeenth century the mineral wealth discovered on the fringe of Stourbridge saw the town move towards industrialisation. The swiftly flowing River Stour was already powering a number of mills engaged in the wool industry and the early stages of iron working. But with the addition of the glass industry, fireclay and coal mining on its borders, Stourbridge became the business centre for Amblecote, Wordsley and Lye.

Arguably, Stourbridge was never a constituent part of the Black Country – although that area was literally next door. For something like one hundred and fifty years the Black Country was regarded by 'outsiders' as not a particularly nice place. Only in recent years with heritage marketing and tourism – and its forced amalgamation into Dudley Borough – has Stourbridge become part of the Black Country.

None the less, because it lay between the countryside of North Worcestershire and South Staffordshire and the industries of the Black Country (also known as 'the Workshop of the World'), Stourbridge was instantly recognised as a desirable place in which to live. Quite apart from some areas where modest houses and basic cottages housed the 'working classes', Black Country businessmen built substantial houses in many parts of the town. Originally these houses were built within easy reach of the railway, and with the advent of the motor car other areas such as Pedmore and Norton saw large houses being built. In some places these large town houses have now been converted to business premises or residential and nursing homes for the elderly as the former owners moved further out of town.

Such was the rapid development of Stourbridge that in 1914 it gained Borough status. Less than fifty years earlier it had been governed by Town Commissioners and then became an Urban District Council. The town's motto 'One Heart One Way' aptly reflected the progressive attitude of its leaders.

And so Stourbridge remained the predominant town in North Worcestershire until 1974 when the authorities of the day, in the face of near-unanimous opposition, reorganised local government. Stourbridge lost its centuries old links with Worcestershire and became part of Dudley County Borough within the newly created West Midlands County.

A few years later when the West Midlands County was (rightfully, said some) dismembered, Dudley became a Metropolitan Borough with a population greater than that of Cardiff. Apart from the Borough Coat of Arms, recovered from a cinema foyer and now embedded in the floor of the Crown Centre, all visible signs of the Borough were effectively extinguished, with a less personal form of local government taking over.

In recent years Stourbridge has suffered further degradation; the ring road (often referred to as 'a folly') was built so close to the town centre as to block any further expansion. Then followed the establishment of the out-of-town shopping 'city' of Merry Hill which led to the demise of several long-established retail businesses.

However, there is still hope. A group of people are actively campaigning for the founding of an elected Town Council (in effect a Parish Council) which, it is hoped, may rekindle the former civic pride. Planners are also looking at re-routing the ring road to allow the town to redevelop.

But whatever the future may hold for Stourbridge and district, the following pictures spanning over a century will recall the days when Stourbridge was a very individual town of character.

Bob Clarke
Michael Reuter
December 2000

# 1

# *Stourbridge Town Centre*

This postcard, posted in Stourbridge on 17 October 1907, was one of many seaside-style cards sent from the town. Sadly, few such cards exist today. This design was printed in vast numbers and supplied throughout the country with local retailers having the location overprinted. In this one the invitation to Stourbridge is printed on a drum. The card was designed by a firm from Fife in Scotland.

In the nineteenth century Stourbridge was an extremely prosperous market town where the coal, iron, clay and glass industries met the agricultural industry of north Worcestershire. In 1872 the town held its first agricultural show with a huge castellated archway being built across the road at the junction of the High Street and Market Street. According to reports, visitors came from all over the country with the social high spot being when the Show President, Viscount Cobham of Hagley, presided over a sumptuous dinner for four hundred people in a marquee. Over £1,000 worth of prizes were distributed.

Without doubt the most photographed feature of Stourbridge in the heyday of postcards was the area around the town clock. Apart from photographs there were painted pictures such as this (*c.* 1903) which appeared to have turned Lower High Street into a level road!

This card puts the locality into a more realistic setting, *c.* 1910. An open-top deck tram is coming up Lower High Street while the police constable appears oblivious to the fact that he is standing on one of the rails!

Only a few years separate these pictures. Above, the bottom of High Street *c.* 1905. To the right is the ironmongers firm of Leadbetter Brothers who, at the time, proclaimed 'Established over a Century'. In the background, a solitary policeman stands at the deserted road junction. The clock reads 3.45 and as the shop is closed it may have been half-day closing or maybe a Sunday afternoon. The flags on two buildings on the lower image could date the picture to 1911 – the date of King George V's coronation.

On 22 June 1911 the town centre was packed with people to watch a parade celebrating the coronation of King George V. Unlike today's Stourbridge Carnival, bunting could not be stretched across the street because of the overhead power lines for the trams. None the less, many of the shops flew a variety of flags. Behind the band is a horse-drawn fire engine. On the left can be seen part of the Old Bank (London City & Midland Bank).

This is the original bank building. Eventually it was rebuilt to its present appearance as the Yorkshire Bank at the junction of High Street and Coventry Street.

The bottom end of High Street, with an open-top tram approaching, *c.* 1914.

*Below*: A remarkably clear and detailed photograph taken around the same period. The building on the left is the Talbot Hotel, once the town's principal coaching inn. As far as local business people and social events were concerned, it was the place to be seen. Note the ornate gas lamps over the carriage entry and the hotel entrance.

Two more scenes captured in impressive detail, *c.* 1920. Above, it is fortunate the tram is leaving the High Street, otherwise the window cleaner whose handcart and ladders are almost on the line would not have been very popular. Below, a scene at 5.20 p.m. with paper sellers in action. The Central Hotel and Dining Rooms stand on the corner of Market Street and beyond the hotel in the High Street is Freeman, Hardy & Willis, while next door is a branch of the Dudley tobacconists A. Preedy & Sons. The rebuilt Old Bank is on the extreme left.

The imposing shop front of E.E. Hawkeswood at the junction of the High Street and New Street. Hawkeswood's periodically changed the signwriting on the wall – at one time it was 'Clothiers and Silk Mercers', then 'Funerals Completely Furnished' and then 'Costumier and Silk Mercer'.

The town centre with Market Street a one-way street, *c.* 1960. Note the temporary traffic island, Hawkeswood's had long since disappeared with the site being occupied by gardens at what is now the entrance to the Crown Centre.

While there are a number of building façades in the centre of the High Street which have changed little over the past seventy years, the top end of the High Street has seen many changes – not least where the ring road was cut through. Above, a scene looking down the High Street early in the twentieth century and below, the same area in about 1930, much of which was eventually demolished to make way for the ring road. The cars have been identified as (left to right) a Ford Popular, an Austin 'Heavy' 12, an Austin 16 and an Austin 7.

The High Street looking down from its junction with Foster Street on the right and overlooked by the decorative façade of Bordeaux House and a lamp-post in the middle of the road. This picture was taken in the early 1930s when the High Street carried two-way traffic.

A crowded High Street with a one-way traffic system, c. 1950. The Royal Exchange public house is on the left while a little further down is the passageway leading to the Kings Cinema in New Road, the entrance to which is marked on a board with 'Kings' written on it.

A rare and highly detailed postcard scene of High Street in the late 1920s. In the centre of the picture is the Royal Exchange. Next door is the F.J. Barnes 'North Worcestershire Garages' and there is an intriguing single-seat sports car parked outside the premises of Hall & Co. Next door up from the Royal Exchange is Temperance House, but by the time the picture below was taken in the 1960s the building had changed ownership. Hall & Co.'s shop had had a facelift while Halliwell's shop had been sold.

High Street with the stone setts road surface clearly visible, *c.* 1918. In the centre is the public library bearing the large sign 'Exhibition'. The lamp standard at the junction of Church Road (left) and Hagley Road (right) was replaced by the war memorial.

The Horse & Groom public house (extreme left) beyond which was the garage of Weaver & Co. with its AA and RAC signs. The pub was demolished to make way for St John's Road and the imposing property with the arched display windows was later demolished to make way for the ring road.

Two pictures showing how little the surroundings have changed over the years in part of High Street. Above, a scene thought to be from around 1914 with shops on the right identified as Howard J. Davies and Merrifield. In the middle distance (right) is the post office. Below is an early afternoon scene from the 1950s, with most of the upper-storey façades still unchanged and when many families still lived 'over the shop'.

This postcard of the early 1900s shows that properties in the Lower High Street had magnificent frontages – a far cry from the appearance of many today. Willimott's shop and the newsagents next door had ornate lanterns and on the wall of the building on the corner of the side street are tenants' names, one of which was the Old Edwardian Club founded in 1898.

Some premises had been demolished to make way for The Scala at which the film of the Dempsey–Carpentier boxing match was shown. Beyond the cinema was Regency House, next door to which was Madame Barlow's hairdressers.

An early photograph of a flag-bedecked Lower High Street, late 1800s. In the background is King Edward VI School and the headmaster's house. The houses next to the school were demolished to make way for an assembly hall in the early 1930s and a side vehicular entrance from Lower High Street. It is thought the flags marked a celebration of Queen Victoria's reign, probably her Jubilee year in 1887.

King Edward VI School, early 1900s. The white building was removed in the mid-1920s to make room for extensions to the school.

Around fifty years separate these two scenes of the Lower High Street – the only major change being the appearance of King Edward VI School's new assembly hall.

Lower High Street had very much its own character and was almost a shopping area in its own right. Indeed, it was once said it was an individual community as, similarly, in the High Street, Market Street and Coventry Street, shop owners lived above their premises. Cooke Ltd are described above the shop window as 'dispensing, family and agricultural chemists'. They were better known as Cooke's Pure Drug Stores and at one time had a number of branches in the Midlands including one in Kinver village.

Lower High Street in the 1920s, heralding the arrival of motor vehicles – one of which is sharing the highway with a horse-drawn milk float and a handcart. To the left is a branch of the Sunshine Laundry and, a little further down the road, a pawnbrokers.

Until the River Authority (at this time it was the Upper Stour Valley Main Sewerage Board) carried out extensive dredging and clearance work, there were times when the River Stour flooded and closed Lower High Street at the borough boundary with Amblecote. Floods isolated the town from traffic coming in from Wolverhampton and Brierley Hill unless by extensive detours. In this scene (left) in 1928 the Stourbridge Workshops for the Blind were swamped and a few years later the ground floors of scores of shops, offices and homes were flooded once again.

At the bottom of the Lower High Street area were a number of humble cottages, 'and in this scene from 1928 ladders and planks were the only way this young family could get in and out of their home. This flood occurred on 1 and 2 June when 3.73 inches of rain fell in only twelve hours – and no-one had even heard of global warming in those days!

Early in the last century Market Street above had a distinctly semi-derelict air despite being close to a prosperous market with the only bright spot being the Victorian mass of the Town Hall. The inn to the right (selling Wordsley Ales and Stout) and the rest of the properties were eventually demolished and the road widened.

On the wall of the pub (roughly on the corner of Talbot Street), old posters seem to have attracted the vandals. On the extreme left, on the corner of Bell Street, is the original Bell Hotel (later to be rebuilt over a row of modern shops). With the widening of Market Street new purpose-built shops were constructed and it was not long before the area rivalled the popularity of the High Street as a shopping area.

Market Street at the corner of New Road, *c.* 1900. The trees on the left stood on the edge of a field – next to St Thomas's Church – on which the church hall was built in 1914. The houses on the right still stand although the corn stores (pictured below) on the corner of Greenfield Avenue was demolished when the ring road was built. Stourbridge Corn Stores was a thriving concern and served a wide area including numerous farms and stables for over fifty years before being flattened by progress. The picture below dates from around 1905.

Stourbridge Town Hall in Market Street was not (and still is not) everyone's dream of an architectural masterpiece although when it was built to commemorate Queen Victoria's Jubilee it was the height of architectural fashion. Over the years it has hosted many prestigious events, and with modern extensions and meeting rooms added when the adjoining Crown Centre was built (plus refurbishment of the Hall itself) it remains an extremely popular venue. With its large stage, the hall put on (and still does) many shows and concerts and in the 1920s the promoter of one show, J. Howard Bennet, brought *The Earl and the Girl* from the Lyric Theatre, London, for two nights.

A promotional postcard for the show was either posted direct to known theatre-goers or hand-distributed around Stourbridge and the surrounding district.

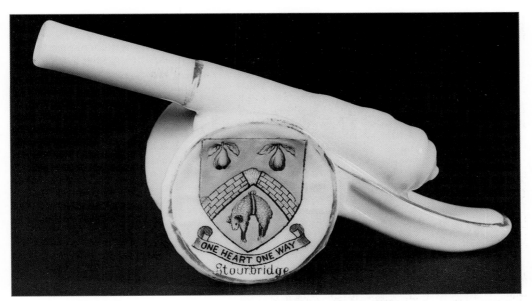

One of the many china ornaments which were popular among local people as well as visitors during late Victorian and early Edwardian times. Why the Stourbridge coat of arms should find its way on to a cannon is puzzling as the town had few warlike tendencies other than a few Civil War skirmishes in the countryside, well away from the town. This ornament (apparently there were a vast number of different designs) was believed to have been made by a pottery in what is now Platts Crescent, Amblecote.

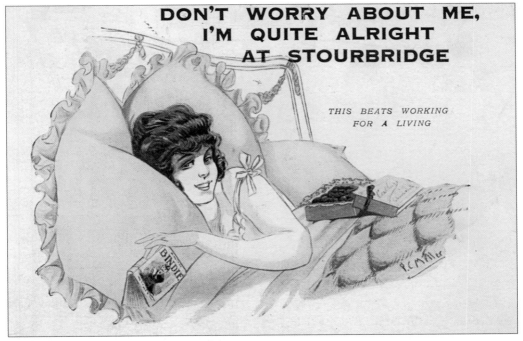

Another card from the days when Stourbridge had a substantial number of holidaymakers apart from people visiting relatives.

Market Street, *c.* 1960. Today, forty years on, this street scene has changed very little. The Stourbridge Institute building (extreme left) is a popular venue for snooker, billiards, bridge or just socialising. Sadly, Stourbridge has lost much of its reputation as a higher quality shopping area. Some say this is because of the arrival of the Merry Hill Centre at Brierley Hill – others say it is a combination of that together with less attention being paid to Stourbridge when it became part of the Dudley Metropolitan Borough Council, resulting in a loss of civic pride.

# 2

# *The Pub Scene*

Stourbridge was no different from any other town of similar size in that it had a large number of public houses – some well-run and others of a more dubious character. One of the older pubs was the Star Inn, High Street. Although shown on an 1837 town map it was thought to have been in existence much earlier. It was described as 'one of the better class houses' and regarded as 'a very sober house' with the barmaids 'standing for no nonsense'. Over the years the building was extended and later reduced in size. In more recent times the premises were converted to shops, one of which was Douglas Watchmakers and Jewellers.

For generations the Star and Garter quenched the thirsts of people after tennis, bowls and other activities in the adjoining Mary Stevens Park. When built it was one of the largest licensed premises in the district. The picture above was taken in the early twentieth century when stabling and livery services were available whereas that below was taken some fifty years later – note the mini-island replacing the old gas lamp that also doubled as a finger post. The property closed down as a traditional pub and became something of a nightclub for a short time before it was wrecked by a fire. It is now a convenience store. The building has lost all its previous character and has been made worse by what many feel is an unsympathetically designed extension.

The Star and Garter licensee in this picture was Thomas Griffin, seen arriving with a cartload of Atkinson's bottled beer.

Bordeaux House, on the corner of Foster Street and High Street, was where Rutland's ran possibly the district's largest off-licence (as well as being wine importers) for many years.

Possibly one of the oldest photographs in existence of High Street is this picture of the Coach & Horses Inn c. 1870. Immediately to the left was a passageway (which still exists) leading to the inn's stables and on to what was known as Angel Street. The building also housed a butcher's shop which, a few years later, was moved to the far end of the block with the pub being sited next to the passageway. In later years, the wooden Alhambra Theatre was built in Barlow's Yard (a site now occupied by the post office depot) with its ticket office and entrance in the passageway. The theatre's proprietor, Mrs Patch, redeveloped the old gabled building with a new Coach & Horses. The inn was eventually demolished with a somewhat characterless building taking its place.

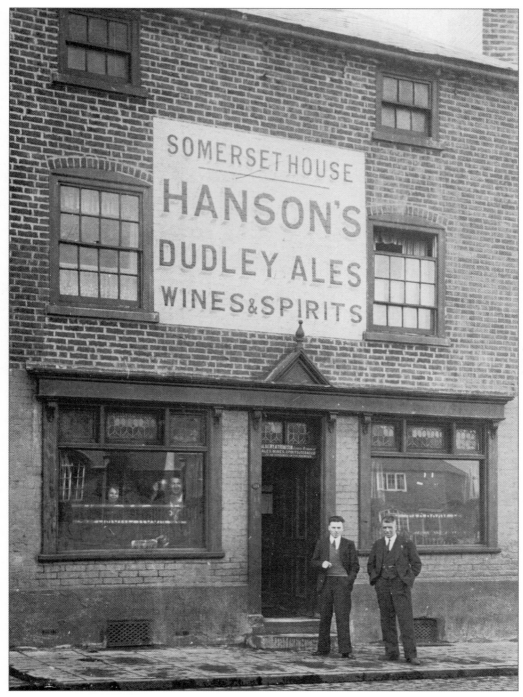

Although there is no record as to how this pub in Enville Street came by the grand sounding name of Somerset House it was well known for one special reason . . . for years there were reports of ghostly happenings in the room on the right of the picture.

A superb nineteenth-century photograph of the 'Tantivy Stage' outside the Old King's Head Inn waiting to depart on its thrice-weekly journey to Birmingham with one passenger already on board. How this service came by its name seems to have been lost with the passage of time. However, we are fortunate to know that the licensee pictured behind the horse is William Vale who is about to load a wicker basket, while the famous stagecoach driver of the time, Jake Gardner, sits proudly aloft. The 'Tantivy Stage' was also a Royal Mail Coach – hence the licence No. VR (Victoria Regina) 9318. The 'Tantivy Stage' left Stourbridge at 10 a.m. every Monday, Thursday and Saturday calling at Cradley, Halesowen and Rowley. Much of its journey was on the turnpike road between Hagley, Halesowen and Birmingham. It is recorded that one stopping place was at the New Inn, Halesowen, where the licensee Betty Taylor was said to brew the finest ales in the district.

This splendid picture is of 'mine host' Frank Matthews, licensee and brewer of the Royal Exchange, Enville Street. He had a brother who owned a fish and chip shop (also in Enville Street) and another brother who was the pianist in the days of silent films at the King's Hall.

Another coaching inn (sadly no photographs of stagecoaches at the Talbot Hotel seem to have survived) was the Bell Hotel, Market Street. This badly faded photograph of unknown date seems to indicate this stagecoach was a much larger vehicle than the 'Tantivy Stage' as it had a team of four horses. Judging from the items on its roof-rack it was heavily laden and may have been a long-distance coach. Stourbridge has always been a major route centre with centuries-old roads radiating out to Worcester (for London), Birmingham, Bridgnorth (for Wales) and Wolverhampton (for the north).

One of the most imposing frontages of any public house in the district was that of the Seven Stars near Stourbridge Junction station. Happily, its frontage has remained virtually unchanged. Why it was built on such a grand scale remains something of a mystery as the residential areas beyond the railway had yet to be built. Presumably it was built to capitalise on trade from passengers leaving the railway station as there was little in the way of industry in the vicinity and little passing trade.

ecause Stourbridge was an important market town prior to the Industrial Revolution and with the arrival of the
lack Country industries on its doorstep by the early 1800s, travelling players used to visit the town and set up
heir tents (usually near public houses). One such venue was Barlow's Yard (at the rear of today's post office) and
onveniently close to the Coach & Horses Inn. According to a feature in the *County Express* some fifty years ago
here was also evidence that there had been 'an establishment' known as the Theatre Royal – probably housed in
 converted barn or in a marquee. Sometime in the 1880s two travelling showmen came to Stourbridge and built
he Alhambra where the Post Office depot now stands. After the proprietor died, his widow Eliza Patch ran it for a
me. Following her death the theatre was bought by experienced actor Douglas Phelps and his wife who managed
 with considerable success. With the advent of moving pictures, Mr Phelps bought a projector and showed films,
ut eventually returned to live shows and the Alhambra became a popular venue for music hall and variety. Faced
ith growing competition from local cinemas it closed down, with the building later being condemned and then
emolished. But the Alhambra had its claim to fame . . . among the budding stars who trod the boards were Lye-
orn actor Sir Cedric Hardwicke and singer Gracie Fields.

ne of the Alhambra's more off-
eat marketing ploys was this
icture of a London and North
Vestern Railway engine
Velocipede', 1904. On the
everse were details of a
orthcoming show. Considering
tourbridge was served by the
reat Western Railway, the
hoice of an LNWR engine – or
ndeed an engine of any kind –
eemed an odd way of
romoting a show.

Under Mr and Mrs Phelps's ownership the Alhambra had some prosperous times. No doubt some of the success was owing to their theatrical experience. They exploited several areas of publicity such as the original postcard (previous page) and paying a gypsy family to advertise the shows on their caravan as they worked their way round the area. Mr Phelps also made use of his van with the patriotic slogan 'Two Things Always On Top' on a painting of the Union Jack, the Alhambra and the word 'Phelps'.

# 3

# *Work & Worship*

Pictures of individual traders in Stourbridge of ninety years or more ago are extremely rare. One which has survived is this publicity postcard of Harry Rowley of Worcester Street, Stourbridge, seen outside his premises presumably with his young son. The sign above the doorway reads: 'H. Rowley, Carpenter & Coffin Maker, Property Repairs Promptly Attended, Funerals Completely Furnished'.

A vast array of Victorian glass globes and shades for gas lights, decorative tiles and toilet brushes form the shop window display of R. Dudley of 120 Lower High Street, Stourbridge, who also sold 'oil paint & colours, zinc sheet, spouting, etc.'

Above is William Tansey, 'poulterer and fruiterer' of 55 High Street, Stourbridge, *c.* 1910. Regrettably no more detail of either the family or the business has come to light.

This undated promotional postcard by E.J. Davies of 65 High Street advised customers he had taken delivery of 'a full range of Two Steeples Unshrinkable Underclothing for Winter Wear'.

A well known gents' outfitters in the inter-war years was Wilkins of High Street. Unfortunately the name of the person in the doorway is not known – could it have been Mr Wilkins?

Readers can judge for themselves which shop has the most character. Above, a photograph of Hilton's Booteries, boot and shoe retailers and makers of 68 High Street, with its distinctive hanging lanterns, *c.* 1914. Below, White's tailors shop front at 82 High Street forms a sharp contrast with its Christmas gift display, *c.* 1960.

The workforce at W.J. Turney & Co., *c.* 1914. The company owned a large tannery in Mill Street, Stourbridge. The company head, William Jonadab Turney, bought the tannery, which also produced parchment and glue, from Joseph Pitman (whose monument is in Oldswinford church). The Turney family were also involved in leather tanning in Nottingham where Mr Turney's brother John became Mayor and Sheriff of Nottingham, later being knighted. Mr Turney took an active political interest from the time he came to Stourbridge in 1867. In 1871 he was elected Chairman of the Town Commissioners (before Stourbridge became an Urban District Council) and Chairman of the Upper Stour Valley Main Drainage Board. He became Chairman of the Stourbridge Press Co. which took over the then ailing Brierley Hill newspaper, the *County Express*, and brought it to Stourbridge as a Conservative newspaper to challenge the influence of the *Advertiser* (later to become the *County Advertiser*) which, as a Liberal newspaper, had a huge circulation (for those days) in Kingswinford, Brierley Hill, Cradley Heath and Old Hill. As the Liberal cause waned so did the *County Advertiser* and the *County Express* became one of Britain's largest selling weekly newspapers. Mr Turney's company donated £1,000 to the building of the Town Hall. He founded the Stourbridge Volunteer Fire Brigade and obtained the lease of the Holloway End ground (Amblecote) from the Earl of Stamford and Warrington (Enville Hall) for Stourbridge Cricket Club. The firm continued until 1957 when it was forced out of business by the use of plastics in place of leather. Mr Turney, who was originally from Boston, Lincolnshire, lived at Park Hill, Love Lane, Oldswinford, and died at Heath House in 1895 aged fifty-four.

Stourbridge War Memorial was financed by public subscription in memory of those who fell in the First World War and was erected outside the public library in 1923. It was designed by Ernest Pickford and unveiled by the Earl of Coventry on 16 February 1923.

A Remembrance Day service a few years after the memorial was erected. The memorial was moved to Mary Stevens Park to make way for the all-consuming ring road.

St John's church, which stands close to the town railway station and ring road, was built in 1860 at a cost of £4,000. It had a narrow escape from destruction on 5 April 1908. Just as the congregation had arrived and the service was about to begin a choir member saw smoke coming from the chancel roof above the vestry. Prompt action by the local volunteer fire brigade meant that the fire was contained to a small section of roof. Contemporary reports say the brigade remained at the scene until the late evening as a precaution.

Regarded by many as a classic example of Georgian church architecture, St Thomas's church in Market Street was completed in 1736. For a time during the eighteenth century the vicars combined their church duties with those of being headmasters of King Edward VI School. The church hall was built in 1914.

The corrugated-iron sheeting of the old church in Glebe Lane, Norton, was later replaced by a modern brick-built church (below) on the opposite side of the road. Dwindling attendances led to the closure of the church which eventually became a chapel of rest owned by a local funeral director, whose offices are now in the house at the extreme right of the picture.

# 4

# *Parks & Leisure*

Greenfield Gardens (named after a large house nearby) on the corner of Greenfield Avenue and Heath Street was bought for the town in 1901. For many years it was a popular spot for Sunday afternoon and summer evening strolls, meeting friends, playing bowls and listening to the regular band concerts. This view is of the gardens not long after their opening. The area was formerly known as Burnt Oak Field.

The bandstand (above) in Greenfield Gardens and the fountain (below) were donated by Walter Jones, the first Chairman of Stourbridge Urban District Council (1894–8). He was the proprietor of one of the area's largest companies, Jones & Attwood. Although the area was always known as Greenfield Gardens, every postcard of this period describes it as Promenade Gardens. In latter times the gardens fell into disrepair and have degenerated into scraggy turf, a few trees and a night-time haunt for less desirable elements.

Once the envy of many local authorities, the gates of Mary Stevens Park (modelled on those of Buckingham Palace) and their imposing pillars were kept in pristine condition by the former Stourbridge Borough Council Parks Department. Today they are a sad reflection of their former glory as are the park's flower beds and parkland owing to less maintenance and the attention of vandals. As Stourbridge grew in size and importance, the council offices and chamber in Market Street became too small, so the council extended the former Studley Court in the grounds of the park to accommodate staff and provide a larger council chamber.

There's something of a mystery surrounding this picture. From wording on the banner it appears to have been an award won by the young choir who had entered the CETS (could that be the Church of England Temperance Society?) Band of Hope singing competition. But which church was it? And when?

Another mystery photograph – the only identification on this photograph are the words 'The Imps'. Obviously it was a group of young people doing their bit for a charity carnival. But was the float entered in the Corbett Hospital Fête or Stourbridge Carnival?

# 5

# *Schooldays*

Stourbridge has a number of fine schools but for centuries the premier spot was held by King Edward VI School. Although founded in 1552, the school had a much earlier predecessor on the same site in the form of Chantry School, which was closed by Henry VIII during his onslaught on the Catholic Church. This picture was taken in about 1933 shortly after the assembly hall had been opened.

This postcard probably did not impress the school or any former pupils. Its phrase 'Grammar School' made no reference to its royal origins and the so-called coat of arms bore no resemblance to the school's badge (the Tudor Arms). All in all the only correct information on the card was the photograph of the school taken in the early 1900s!

Forms V2a and V2b with several well-known families (some still in the Stourbridge area) represented. Those identified are back row, left to right: Leslie Compton, Cecil Chance, -?-, -?-, Herbert Bowen, -?-, Stan Edwards, Henry Worton, ? Thorpe, -?-, -?-, -?-. Middle row: Bill Davies, Kenneth Bolton, ? Cotton, Gerald Pope, Mr C.V. 'Tilt' White, Mr J. 'Bodger' Timbrell (senior chemistry master), Albert Ray, ? Canning, ? Dodd, ? Pitt, ? Williams. Front row: Bill Dudley, Ralph Dangerfield, ? Vale, Stanley Eveson, Albert Genner, Reg Whitworth, ? Thompson, -?-, Dennis Morgan, Howard Green. By all accounts in later years Mr White was a remarkable man. Although having a disability with his right arm, he was a formidable badminton player in the Cradley Heath and District Churches Badminton League in the late 1930s and was still playing badminton at the Stourbridge Institute when he was eighty-two! The Stourbridge Old Edwardian Club with premises in Drury Lane (off Market Street) is now over one hundred years old and has built up a considerable archive of material relating to the school. It is always happy to receive further memorabilia.

This photograph is thought to be of the King Edward VI School's second XI football team of 1919. In later years, football at the school gave way to Rugby Union in which all the school teams enjoyed consistent success. For many years, the school playing fields were off Vicarage Road, Amblecote, and were large enough to accommodate three rugby pitches. Later the land was sold for housing development and the school acquired land alongside Swinford Road, Oldswinford. The team members pictured are (standing): Wood, Robinson, Rowley, Mr Scholes, Turner, Price, Mason; (seated): Wright, Wooldridge, Tate, Simister, Fletcher.

The 1951/2 season was a memorable one for Stourbridge Football Club for that was the year they won the Birmingham Combination League Championship. Pictured above with the championship shield, the players and officials are: Back row, left to right: George Jones, Jack Guest, W. March, Cyril Davies, Gerald Hill, ? Corbett, Dennis Powell, F. Perry, H. Thompson, Gordon Davis, J. Harrington. Middle row: J. Stinton (trainer), Fred Deakin, Ron Page, S. Bazeley, Jock Poyner, Ted Rowberry, W. Kendrick (physio). Front row: Fred Haycock, Eric Hipkiss, Stan Dunn, Jim Condie.

In 1900 cycling was a major recreation and this picture is of the Stourbridge Cycling Club in that year. The club was founded in 1892 at the Vine Inn. The president was the Earl of Dudley and vice-presidents included many of the town's leading businessmen. An even earlier mention of organised cycling can be found in the 1886 *Stourbridge Directory* – namely the Excelsior Bicycle Club with W.J. Turney as president and based at the Mitre Inn.

After Studley Court (later to become the Stourbridge Borough Council offices) ceased being a private residence it was converted into a somewhat upmarket boarding school for girls. With 'special attention being given' (according to the prospectus) to physical training, the young ladies underwent a daily drill supervised by a former sergeant of the 11th Hussars. Among a wide variety of sport there was cricket, the only language spoken at mealtimes was French and supervised swimming took place in the lake. The school's prospectus told parents of would-be pupils: 'Students are under the personal care of the Principal who has had much experience and whose aim is to give a first-class modern education combined with the moral tone and social culture of a refined home life.' This picture appeared in the prospectus as a marketing aid.

By the time the young ladies of Studley Court had finished their education they must have been exceptionally fit. Apart from daily 'drill sessions', the park's lake was the school's swimming pool – it was no doubt much cleaner in those days.

Studley Court had its own farm and sanatorium as seen in this undated postcard.

# 6

# *At Your Service*

For many years King Edward VI School had an Army Cadet Force Corps. This photograph, believed to have been taken seventy or more years ago, comprises members of the band with their uniforms in the same style as those of the British Army during the First World War. We are fortunate that we have obtained the names of every boy. Back row, left to right: Milner, Hodgetts, Brooks, Warner, Boucher, Cork. Middle row: Ince, Gough, Brazier, Berry, Ford, Page. Front row: Carlyle, Horton, Shaw, Watkins, Cowley, Ward, Pearson, Holloway. Many years later, the Corps became part of the Combined Cadet Force which was established in public and grammar schools throughout England and Wales to gain Army, Navy and Air Force Cadets. In Stourbridge the Corps remained solely as an army unit and was attached to the Worcestershire Regiment. Many of its former members served with distinction during the Second World War with a number having joined in pre-war days as regulars. Around forty years ago it was disbanded – the only remaining Combined Cadet Force in the district is at Oldswinford School.

Within a short time of Baden-Powell introducing 'Scouting for Boys' several scout troops (now called groups) were formed in Stourbridge and the surrounding district. One of the largest was at St Thomas's church and this photograph was taken at the rear of the church, *c.* 1930. The towers of the fire station and the town hall can be seen in the background. Two people have been identified: Ron Sparks (of Peewit Patrol) is standing extreme right back row. The scoutmaster (now called leader) was Chris Gittins, who rose to national fame as the irascible Walter Gabriel in the BBC radio series *The Archers*.

A picture from the early days of scouting. Although the troop is unidentified it is particularly significant in that Baden-Powell is pictured in the centre of the middle row. Sitting next to him is Isaac Nash, who was Stourbridge Urban District Council chairman from 1900 to 1905.

Those were the days! No shortage of policemen here. The photograph of all available officers in the Stourbridge Division was taken possibly on the day of a Government Inspection on 27 June 1912. There are fifty-three men on the photograph and it is reasonable to suppose that this was not the full strength, because of holidays, urgent inquiries or sick leave. Today's manning level is around forty, even though the population has more than trebled. The man in the centre of the front row is Superintendent Thomas Hinde and on his left is Inspector Samuel Danks. On Inspector Danks's left is Sergeant William Brown. In the first (standing) row, eighth from the left, is Constable Albert Milner (brother of Constable Walter Milner whom we featured in our first book in 1997). The photograph was taken in the rear yard of the station. The high wall to the left shielded the prisoners' exercise yard. Beyond this were the cells from which steps led up into the court room.

Both these photographs were taken in 1929. On the left is Constable 169 William Henry Thomas Wall who had joined shortly before the photograph was taken in the yard of the former Worcestershire County Police headquarters in Castle Street, Worcester (the headquarters later moved to Hindlip Hall, Fernhill Heath, Worcester). He was a native of Great Witley and served at Redditch, Stourbridge (13 October 1930 to 20 November 1931), Worcester, Bromsgrove and then returned to Redditch. He died in 1994. Below is Constable 308 Norman Hand, a native of Wollaston. He never served in Stourbridge although is it feasible he may have been there for a short time as recruits sometimes received their initial training at Stourbridge before being posted. Otherwise he could have been trained at Worcester before being sent on his first posting to Halesowen on 20 February 1920. He later served at Romsley, Redditch and Wythall. He retired in 1952 and is believed to have died in 1992. Certainly in 1990/91 he had relatives in Wollescote, his wife having come from Lye.

*Opposite*: A photographer's studio was the setting for this carefully posed picture. It would be interesting to know what special occasion warranted such a photograph. On the left is Sergeant 237 William Brown and Constable 253 James Broad is on the right. The photograph is also interesting as the officers are wearing a new head dress, the 'pill-box' hats in the group photograph (previous page) having been discarded. It is thought the photograph was taken during the First World War when both men were serving at Lye, which was part of the Stourbridge Division. Both men retired at Lye on 30 June 1919. William Brown came from Kidderminster and before joining the police in 1887 he was a gardener. Before coming to Lye he served all over the county and was promoted Sergeant in 1893. James Broad was a native of Dodderhill near Droitwich, and was a shoemaker before joining the police in 1890 and serving at Blockley, Moseley and Selly Oak (before those communities became part of Birmingham), Stourbridge, Wribbenhall and Lye.

When it was built Stourbridge police station was one of the most imposing buildings in town. Coupled with an accommodation block for single officers, its size reflected the growth in population of the division. The magistrates court and offices were built at the far end of the building at the same time. In those days and until the creation of the West Midlands Police it was a Worcestershire Constabulary divisional headquarters. Becoming part of the West Midlands force it became a sub-division of Halesowen within the 'J' Division (Dudley). With yet more reorganisation it is now what is called a sector station with its own inspector.

day's modern fire station at Parkfield is a sharp contrast to the late nineteenth century when fire-fighting services ere in the hands of a number of insurance companies. If fire broke out on your premises and you were not insured en you had big problems! In 1879 local industrialist Henry Turney established a Volunteer Fire Brigade and a ar later a horse-drawn fire engine with a steam-powered pump was bought. When the town hall was built it corporated a fire station and in 1926 a purpose-built station was opened alongside the town hall in Smithfield d opened by the Marquess of Cambridge. Until the outbreak of the Second World War it was maintained by luntary subscription after which all brigades came under government control as the National Fire Service. In 48 it became part of the Worcestershire County Fire Brigade and later was amalgamated into the West Midlands igade. In this picture of the town brigade, *c.* 1914, some of the officers have been identified. Back row (extreme ft on the ladder), H. Bingham. Middle row, left to right: -?-, Fred Griffin, J. Steele, W. Meredith, -?-, -?-, Wightman. Front row: -?-, -?-, C. Berry, P. Harper, Capt. C. Walker, -?-, -?-, ? Round. With stone setts as a road rface rather than asphalt, travel on the engine would have been a bone-shaking experience – note the solid tyres!

Fireman Fred Griffin strikes a dramatic pose in this studio portrait. What special event prompted this? It is certainly equal to the publicity photographs of showbusiness stars!

From the same era (and possibly from the same studio) is this photograph of Mr Nash (there is no note of his rank) and Capt. Walker (right). It would be interesting to know what the medals were awarded for – Mr Nash has one with a cross embroidered on the ribbon; was that for an act of gallantry?

Stourbridge Fire Brigade attended some large outbreaks outside the town and occasionally assisted the independent volunteer brigade of Lye which was founded in 1909. One major fire they attended (recorded in *Kinver in Old Photographs: A Second Selection*) was at Enville Hall in the days of the Stourbridge horse-drawn steam-powered pump. Another big fire attended was at Prestwood House, formerly one of the homes of the Foley family. The house had been bought by the Staffordshire, Wolverhampton and Dudley Joint Committee for the treatment of tuberculosis, and was being converted into a sanatorium when fire broke out on Sunday 22 January 1922: the building was gutted. It is thought the fire had been smouldering for some time after workmen had finished for the weekend. Pictured above is the house when it was privately owned and (below) a day or two after the fire with some Stourbridge firemen still on duty damping down.

The Stourbridge brigade also fought a blaze at Hagley Hall in the early hours of Christmas Eve, 1925. Owing to storm the previous day, telephone lines had been brought down, which caused some delay in raising the alarr Hall staff, villagers and firemen worked desperately to save valuable works of art as well as furniture. Such was th ferocity of the blaze that firemen were on the scene for some time and were accommodated in tents in the hal parkland. In this photograph are, left to right: George Whiteman, Charlie Berry, Tim Rutland, Fred Griffin ar Bill Meredith.

Apart from its success in fighting many spectacular blazes in the area, the Stourbridge brigade was famed throughout the Midlands for its all-round efficiency. This is the Brigade's team which won the National Fire Brigades Union Midland District Mitchell Challenge Shield, *c.* 1927. Pictured are, left to right: Fred Griffin, Bill Meredith, Charlie Berry and George Whiteman. The precise date of the photograph is unknown but it could have been taken shortly after the Smithfield Fire Station (adjoining the town hall) was opened in 1926. At the time of this publication the site of the Smithfield station is an unkempt piece of ground adjacent to the Market Street entrance to the Crown Centre.

Stourbridge post office in the High Street has hardly changed externally since this early 1900s postcard. It was opened in 1895 and the passageway to the right now connects with the ring road. It was also along this passage that the Alhambra theatre was situated.

The postwoman featured here in a studio pose was one of several women recruited to take the place of men who had joined the armed forces in the First World War. Their uniform was massive by today's standards: they had a rubber-hemmed skirt, stout boots, heavy duty topcoat and a broad-brimmed hat. This postwoman has been identified as Mabel Wainwright.

Pictured just before setting out on their rounds are these postmen of around eighty years ago. A number of them have been identified: T. Elcock, A. Chance, R. Jones, H. Bott, J. Walton, S. Curnew, B. Bullock, J. Eveson, W. Barlow, A.H. Brown, H. Stokes, T. Farmer, T.B. George, H. Skelding, T. Chance, F.J. Beddall, H. Clark, D. Cooper, B. Garbett, E. Taylor.

Stourbridge and the surrounding area was one of the biggest population centres in Worcestershire and wa a major recruiting centre for the Worcestershire Regiment. This postcard, taken between 1902 and 190 at the Wednesday Market in Beverley, Yorkshire, shows 'I' Company, 1st Volunteer Battalio Worcestershire Regiment (Stourbridge Company of Cyclists) parading through Beverley High Street whi

in camp locally. The volunteers later became the 7th Battalion Worcestershire Regiment (Territorial Force) in 1908 ('H' Company at Stourbridge) and, after the Second World War, the Territorial Force became the Territorial Army (TA). For years the 'Terriers' had their HQ in Bell Street, Stourbridge, but later moved to a new drill hall and complex at Oldswinford.

Two world wars separate these pictures. Right is Benjamin Noke (or Nock) pictured not long after joining the Royal Flying Corps (the forerunner of the Royal Air Force), in 1914. His rank and occupation in the RFC is unknown but in civilian life he was a coffin maker and obtained his timber from Batham's sawmills, Stourbridge.

Three members of the Oldswinford Home Guard company pictured shortly after joining. Left is Corporal William ('Bill') Baden Powell (no relation!), who eventually became a captain, with Private Bert Perrins and Lance Corporal Ted Roden. Mr Powell was a veteran of the First World War, having lied about his age to volunteer for the Royal Flying Corps and serve as a rear gunner. Later he was Managing Director of Stringer & Sons Ltd, lifting gear manufacturers and Mark Attwood Ltd., chainmakers of Old Hill. Both firms eventually became part of the Lye-based John Folkes Hefo. His home was in Stanley Road, Norton.

# 7

# *The Coming of the Railway*

The first Stourbridge station was built in 1852 to serve the Oxford–Worcester–Wolverhampton line, when a branch line to the town opened in 1879. In 1860 the Stourbridge Railway Company obtained an Act of Parliament to build a line to Lye, Cradley Heath and Old Hill from where branch lines were built to Dudley and to the Midland Railway near Longbridge. When the line opened the station became known as Stourbridge Junction; a few years later the line was extended to Smethwick and Birmingham (Snow Hill). In 1901 the Junction station, which had only two platforms (and a small one for the town service), was handling many extra trains, including London and Cardiff expresses. As a result of this increased traffic a new station was built at its present site and the old station in Junction Road (formerly known as Halfpenny Hall Lane) was demolished in 1905. The photograph was taken not long after the new station opened. Close examination shows a train of four- or six-wheel coaches and an engine probably at one time owned by the OW&W and which may well have been built at a locomotive works adjoining Shrub Hill station, Worcester. In the background Chawn Park can be seen. Today this area is intensively built up. The chimney in the distance could possibly have been at a brickworks. In the foreground a public footpath to the Chawn Park area passes under the railway.

This photograph possibly dates from the 1890s and is of the Town station showing the original footbridge int
Vauxhall Road. In the foreground the lines cross Foster Street which was lowered to enable the line to b
continued down to the goods depot and canal interchange basin at Lower High Street.

onsidering Stourbridge Town station was served by a push-pull coach and engine service from the Junction ation and only had one platform, there seemed to be no shortage of staff in this early twentieth-century hotograph. Some may possibly have come up from the goods depot in Lower High Street for the photo call. The own station was opened at about the same time the main line was opened from Stourbridge to Smethwick and n to Birmingham Snow Hill. At this time the term Junction station was used, as the original station was built to rve the Oxford, Worcester and Wolverhampton route. Both that and the Stourbridge Railway Company were ventually taken over by the Great Western Railway.

*Opposite*: A railway excursion about to leave the Town station, *c.* 1890. Unfortunately there are no details of the ashionably dressed party or their destination.

Two views of Stourbridge Junction Station staff. Above, this image from 1912 of the Stourbridge Junction staff carries no identification of the men although the stationmaster is obviously sitting in the middle of the centre row. In those days only inspectors and stationmasters carried their rank on their hats; everyone else carried the letters GWR. A few years later in the 1920s, inspectors, guards, ticket collectors and porters were clearly identifiable. In both photographs the men in straw boaters are something of a mystery. Could they have been big-wigs from the railway company?

This is a particularly poignant photograph – the departure of a special train taking soldiers from Stourbridge to France during the First World War. For some, this was the last time they saw their home town. The photograph was taken just as the train was about to move off. Close examination shows the blur of the connecting rod which indicates that because of the heavy load the engine's driving wheels were slipping. The platform from which the train was leaving now forms part of the station's car park.

'Who's going to pay for this then?' Because of the steep gradient from the town to the goods yard in Lower High Street it was not unknown for engines and/or wagons to run away. This engine went straight through the office and showered debris on the road, early 1900s. Some runaways were even more destructive . . . on one occasion an engine actually finished up on the pavement and road.

Two contrasting views of the ten-arch viaduct across the Stour Valley. Above, the scene looking toward Stambermill in the early 1900s is vastly different from today, with the Penfields Estate covering the farmland. Below, a dramatic picture of one of the infamous River Stour floods. It was not until extensive dredging and channel improvements were carried out that the danger of flooding became more remote.

Two views of the Town station which used to have a character all of its own. Above, the town 'Dodger' as it was known waits at the platform. These were the days when the station handled a large amount of parcel traffic. The scene below was taken from the footbridge. To the right are the Midland Red double-decker buses on the 130 Birmingham service. The remainder of the bus departure stands were either on part of the station yard or in the forecourt of the bus garage, the roof of which can be seen in the background. At this time the Lower High Street goods depot was still in use.

Platform No. 1 at Stourbridge Junction then (as now) the departure platform for the Town, 1957. The roof of the original station booking office in traditional style can be seen on the right.

An ex-GWR Prairie tank engine taking water prior to leaving for Birmingham Snow Hill. Driver Len Shingles opens the valve for fireman Roy Gwilliam (standing on the tank top) to fill the engine's side tanks. Both photographs are reproduced by courtesy of Kidderminster Railway Museum, Station Approach, Comberton, Kidderminster. The museum is open every weekend throughout the year and on every weekday the Severn Valley Railway is operating. Admission is free.

Stourbridge Engine Shedmaster Mr Doviston, who lived in Witton Street, Norton, is seen second from the right, wearing a bowler hat as a symbol of his rank. With him are shed workmen and two men whose very attire seems to indicate (as in earlier photographs in this chapter) they may have been of some managerial rank. The engine, incidentally, was 3450 *Mauritius* and was one of the same class as the record breaking *City of Truro*. The photograph dates from 1928.

A picture of pure nostalgia for steam buffs – a morning scene in the engine shed at Amblecote with pannier tank engines being steamed up. The shed was opened between 1924 and 1926 and held a maximum of sixty-seven engines. The shed was demolished in the late '60s and the surrounding area was cleared for redevelopment.

This rather aristocratic looking gentleman was GWR Inspector Frederick James Greenslade who was based at Stourbridge Junction for some years.

GWR staff of all grades were famed for their expertise in first aid. The Stourbridge stations were no exception and, by all accounts, regularly won regional and national competitions. Incidentally, the white rock seen in the background is in fact painted stone. GWR staff were noted for this activity – whether it was for safety reasons during darkness or simply that some ex-army officer decided that anything that moved must be saluted and anything that didn't must be painted! Who knows . . .?

# 8

# *Road Transport*

The best known bus and coach operator in the town at one time was Samuel 'Sammy' Johnson whose Supreme Coaches operated from Victoria Street, Stourbridge. This picture shows an all-male party about to leave Stourbridge in about 1918. It is thought Mr Johnson himself was the driver of this solid-tyred charabanc, the unladen weight of which was given as 2 tons 19 cwts. In the background is Stourbridge police station in New Road. Mr Johnson's foray into bus services came to grief when he took on the monopolistic Midland Red. For every bus he ran, the Midland Red put on two, one of which was known as a swinger, which meant they could prevent him from collecting passengers at the more popular stops. There were reports of flaring tempers with the occasional bout of fisticuffs between drivers and conductors. Eventually some order was restored by the government-created traffic commissioners who, inexplicably, gave the Midland Red virtual *carte blanche* on all routes other than where local authorities operated their own fleets. Mr Johnson was forced to admit defeat and from then on concentrated on coach trips. He must have gained tremendous satisfaction from the fact that his coaches were acknowledged to be more reliable, comfortable and cleaner than those of his arch-rival. Certainly, the local Midland Red coaching operation was something of an also-ran.

# BOOK UP NOW — FOR BLACKPOOL ILLUMINATIONS

THE SUMMER IS FAST COMING TO ITS CLOSE, SO TAKE A TRIP AND MAKE THE MOST OF IT WHILST YOU CAN IN

## SAMUEL JOHNSON'S "SUPREME" COACHES

**YOUR SAFETY**

On January 19th, 1929, we advertised that we had obtained

**NO CLAIMS BONUS**

from our Insurance Company

Every year since and **AGAIN THIS YEAR WE HAVE UPHELD THAT RECORD ON ALL VEHICLES**. Without fear of contradiction, we have the finest record for miles around.

**ADVERTISING**

We are prepare to pay clien liberally for wir dow or wall di plays. Apply fo particulars.

| | | |
|---|---|---|
| **MONDAY, SEPTEMBER 26th—** | | |
| 2.30 p.m. NEWNHAM BRIDGE & TENBURY | 3/6 | |
| 6.30 p.m. EVENING TRIP | 1/3 | |
| **TUESDAY SEPTEMBER 27th—** | | |
| 8. 0 a.m. BARMOUTH | 10/- | |
| 2.30 p.m. DROITWICH & WORCESTER | 2/6 | |
| **WEDNESDAY, SEPTEMBER 28th (Cont.)—** | | |
| 6.30 p.m. EVENING TRIP | 1/ | |
| **THURSDAY, SEPTEMBER 29th—** | | |
| 2.30 p.m. MYSTERY TRIP including Tea | 5/ | |
| 6.30 p.m. EVENING TRIP | 1/ | |
| **SATURDAY, OCTOBER 1st—** | | |
| 1. 0 p.m. SPECIAL TWO-DAY TRIP | | |

Samuel Johnson's 'Supreme' fleet of luxury long-distance coaches came into their own from 1945 and, as this advertisement from the *County Express* shows, even as late in the season as September 1949 there was a wide variety of trips available, including two-day seaside breaks. Note the proud claim that they had several years of no insurance claims on their drivers. Pictured above is one of his Maudslay coaches – he took delivery of several in one day.

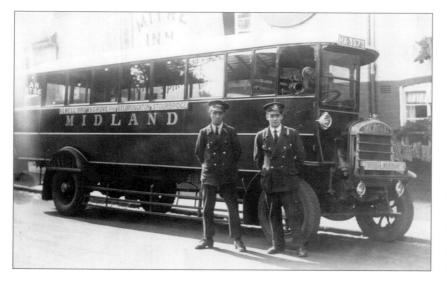

Johnson's arch-enemy, the Midland Red, *c.* 1925. In a posed photograph this Smethwick-registered bus (HA 3573) appears outside the Mitre Inn. The conductor (left) is Eric Smith who lived in South Road, Norton. However, the normally well-tuned bus publicity machine tripped up with this picture for the destination board on the front said 'Stourbridge–Wolverhampton' while on the side of the bus the destination board read 'Hewell, Bromsgrove, Belbroughton, Stourbridge'.

This bus, possibly owned by the Great Western Railway and which ran between Stourbridge, Clent and Belbroughton, caused a major sensation when it skidded and slithered across roadworks near Oldswinford crossroads. Ironically, it happened outside premises which were later to be occupied by the Stourbridge motor and motorcycle engineers Frederick J. Barnes – the same firm that was advertising on the top deck of the bus. It was not many years later that many buses were in use and competition between operators was so intense that it resembled something of a free-for-all.

The changing style of buses is captured here. Above, a double-decker weekend X33 service from Dudley to Stourport approaches Coventry Street, Stourbridge. Below, a 1968 F-registration single-decker was of the same type that was used on the high-speed M5 motorway service between Birmingham and Worcester but was doing more mundane duties on the Stourbridge–Pedmore Fields service. Next to it is an older vehicle on the 240 Cradley Heath route.

The vast area covered by the Midland Red can be judged by this 'until further notice' timetable of all services in the Birmingham area including the Black Country, 1943. The service number on the bus illustration, 144, was the Birmingham–Malvern service.

This scale tramcar (⅜ in to 1 ft) No. 70, a model of the one which ran between the Fish Inn, Amblecote, and Kinver, was built in 1982 by Mr. E. Jackson-Stevens as a Christmas present for his granddaughter who was a tramway enthusiast. Amblecote was where the Kinver Light Railway – a grand name for a tramway – joined the tramway network encompassing the whole of the Black Country, Walsall, Wolverhampton and Birmingham. The line carried huge numbers of people until bus service competition forced its closure in 1930. There was a time when a return ticket to Kinver from the Town Hall Birmingham cost 1s 6d. Although most, if not all, trams travelling through Amblecote were double-deckers, all trams on the Kinver line had to be single-deckers. This was because of the fact that when the completed line was inspected by a government engineer, he said 'neither the line nor its bridges over the Stour and Canal were strong enough to take more than a single-decker'.

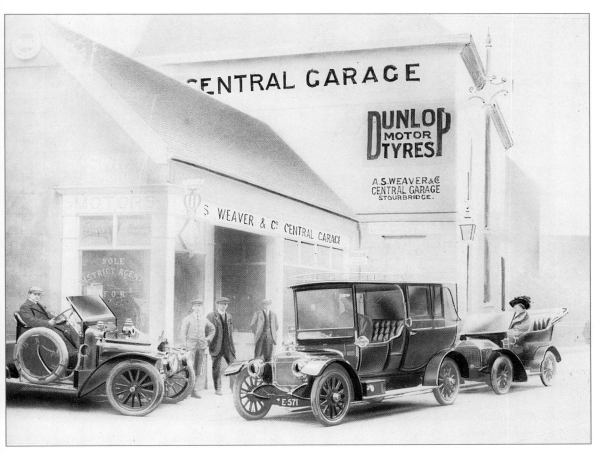

S. Weaver & Co., High Street, trading as Central Garages, was, in its time, one of the oldest established garages in Stourbridge, seen here in about 1920. By virtue of its position between the Black Country and the affluent outlying areas of Norton, Pedmore, Hagley and Clent, cars in Stourbridge tended to be a little more luxurious as this carefully posed publicity picture of the garage shows. During the Second World War the building was converted to a British restaurant, and after this closed the building became a fruit, vegetable and fish market known as 'Housewives' Corner'. This was later demolished to make way for the ring road.

Another long-established town centre garage was that of Frederick 'Freddie' J. Barnes who moved his car and motorcycle business from High Street to Oldswinford, where it traded as North Worcestershire Garage and was a dealer for Humber and Swift cars and cycles. In later years it became a Vauxhall dealership. This dealership eventually moved to what is now probably one of the oldest family-owned garage businesses in Britain, still operated by the Heynes family. The business was featured in our first selection of old photographs of the area.

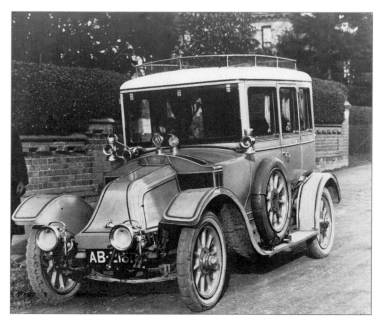

This magnificent machine was a 15.9hp, 2.5 litre Arrol-Johnson car first registered to Jones & Attwood of Titan Works, Stourbridge. The photograph is dated around 1912. This model was introduced at the 1909 motor show and was made in Paisley, Scotland, before production moved to Dumfries in 1913.

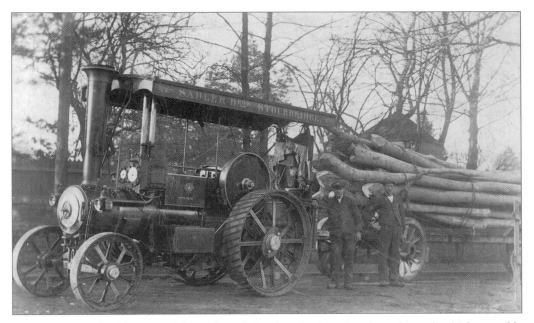

Before the arrival of the powerful petrol- and diesel-engined lorries, the only road vehicles capable of moving heavy loads were steam-powered lorries or traction engines such as this one owned by Sadler Brothers of Stourbridge, pictured here in about 1915 at Batham's timber yard.

This smartly presented light delivery lorry was owned by Saunders & Bowkley Ltd (Ironmongers and Implement Makers). What present vehicle usage legislation would have made of the advertising slogan on the windscreen 'The Leading Ironmongers Phone No. 2 Stourbridge' is another matter . . . but the immaculately clad driver could have argued he could see over the top.

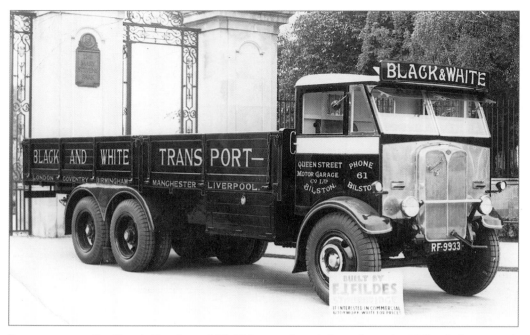

For many years the Stourbridge firm of F.J. Fildes was famed throughout the Midlands for its work on commercial vehicle body construction and body repair work. This early 1930s lorry was an example and is shown on a publicity postcard outside the Mary Stevens Park gates.

Another well-known name in Stourbridge was that of J. Albert Abel, auctioneer, valuer and shipping agent. His earlier offices were in Enville Chambers (possibly in Enville Street) and later moved to Church Road. The posters on the wall were for the P&O (Peninsular & Orient), Cunard and Canadian Pacific shipping lines. It is a reasonable assumption that many local families caught in the economic depression of the early 1930s made use of his services to emigrate to North America, South Africa, Australia or New Zealand. Whether Mr Abel was one of the two men in the car is not recorded.

# 9

# *Urban Expansion*

As Stourbridge's prosperity grew with the expansion of industrial and commercial interests in and around the town, the accompanying increase in population led to surrounding farmland being taken over by housing. Because there was no public or private transport yet, the more affluent (those with a coach and horse) headed out to Norton and Pedmore, while the less wealthy bought terraced villas and cottages. Norton is now an interesting mix of housing some of which dates back to the early to mid-1800s. Almost the whole of Norton is now built up and one of the later areas to have been developed was this dairy farm and house owned by a Mr Edwards and on which the Belbroughton Road estate has now been built. Witton Street can be seen in the background.

From the earliest days of Stourbridge's expansion, Hagley Road has always had a variety of buildings, most of which were built by local business families being within walking distance of the town centre. Apart from the old library and county court there was a mix of terraced cottages and larger detached houses before reaching Oldswinford. This variation in property can be seen in these two postcard scenes, above in 1913, and below c. 1938.

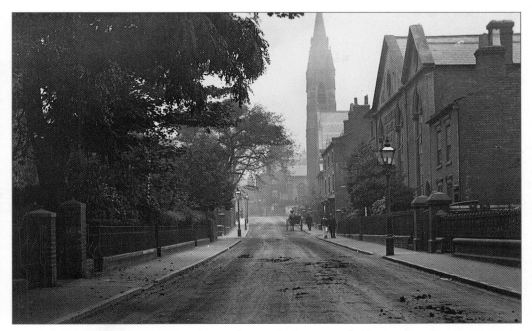

New Road in the early 1900s is a far cry from today's ring road. The scene is dominated by the 130-ft spire of the Catholic church. To the right is the Methodist church and Minister's house – later both were replaced by more modern buildings. Behind the trees on the left were imposing Edwardian and Georgian houses which later became offices and now have the ring road only a few feet from their front doors.

This postcard view of the early 1950s (judging by the type of bus approaching) shows little change other than electric street lighting columns and the rebuilt Methodist church.

Bath Road was another attractive byway close to the town centre later wiped out by the ring road. The first suggestion of public baths was made in 1886 but it was not until 1901 that they were built – even so, Stourbridge was still one of the earliest authorities of a comparable size to have such a facility. An unheated outdoor pool was opened in 1923 and sixteen years later the baths were modernised. During the winter months the indoor pool was covered and the building used for a variety of meetings, dances and an indoor cricket school. The building and most of the houses, plus the Territorial Army HQ in Bell Street, were demolished to make way for the Crystal leisure centre. At the top of Bath Road can be seen the houses in Greenfield Avenue.

Malthouse Row was a group of cottages lying off the Norton Road and opposite Mary Stevens Park lake. Presumably the larger building to the left was the malthouse.

Worcester Street photographed from the end of Market Street, *c.* 1930. To the left is New Road and to the right, Greenfield Avenue. In later years the former public dispensary building on the right became a dance and stage school and subsequently became business offices.

A postcard view of Greenfield Avenue, 1903. This road also saw many fine houses built for families whose business interests were not only in Stourbridge but in neighbouring areas such as Amblecote, Wordsley and Lye. Industrialists from further afield in the Black Country also made their homes in and around Stourbridge as transport links improved.

Apart from today's heavy traffic, Norton Road is another location which has changed little as these two postcard views show. On the left-hand side of the road, large detached and semi-detached houses were built from Victorian times and overlooked farmland. From around 1930 more modest houses were built on the opposite side of the road.

Another area close to the town where upmarket houses put in an appearance was Red Hill. One of its attractions was its easy walking distance to either the Town or Junction railway stations.

Queen's College, Red Hill, was a comparatively short-lived private school owned by a Mr Johnson-Ball. At one time he was the principal of Halesowen Technical College. It offered education for boys and girls from four years of age.

During the seventeenth century the local iron industry began to develop with forges and mills appearing in large numbers on the banks of the swift-flowing River Stour. One family, the Foleys, became all-powerful in this industry with several family members making fortunes which they invested in buying vast estates in Staffordshire, Worcestershire and Herefordshire. They added to their influence and wealth by marrying into other wealthy and titled families. Stourbridge historian and former journalist H. Jack Haden records the fact that the head of the Foley dynasty, Thomas (1616–77), became a noted public benefactor after being impressed by a sermon given by the Puritan, Richard Baxter, on the proper use of wealth. One of his first acts was to found Oldswinford Hospital School (once known as the Bluecoats School) as a charity school for boys of poor families. Much of his huge estate in Pedmore and Stourbridge was retained as part of the school's endowment. With the demise of King Edward VI School as a grammar school and becoming a Sixth Form College some thirty years ago, the Oldswinford School underwent expansion which continues to this day. Its scholastic achievements now rank it among the top schools in Britain.

# 10

# *Oldswinford, Wollaston &*
# *Amblecote*

At the Oldswinford end of Red Hill, the housing stopped abruptly as the road plunged through a sandstone cutting to reach Oldswinford.

An old postcard scene of Hagley Road, Oldswinford, looking from Stourbridge. With no tram lines having been lai[...] this dates the card pre-1900.

Another scene of Oldswinford this time looking towards Stourbridge with Heath Lane to the left just beyond th[...] Waterloo Inn sign. The licensee of this pub was G. Plevy. To the right, judging from the sign, is what appears to b[...] a carriage repair business – this location is now occupied by a filling station forecourt.

The Noke family of 184 Hagley Road, Oldswinford, traded from 1876 until around 1950. This photograph dates from about 1890. George Noke was a noted coffin maker (obtaining his wood from Batham's) and the sign on the building says he could make 'oak or lead coffins' as well as being an upholsterer. The property also boasted the only public weighbridge for miles around and local farmer, Mr Wellbridge, was a regular caller to have his prize bull weighed at a cost of 1d per weighing.

A photograph of the younger Noke generation: from the left, Edgar, Christine and Wilfred.

Mr G.A. Cranage, founder of Cranage's Bakery, Oldswinford, in a posed photograph for a postcard on 16 June 1915. The back of the postcard carries the words 'Down by the Mill Mayflower' – possibly Mayflower was the name of the horse. But what mill was he referring to?

A well-known Oldswinford baker and grocer was Daniel Oakley, one of whose fleet of delivery vans is seen here outside the shop premises.

Stourbridge Model Laundry, Oldswinford, was founded in 1897 and prospered for many years. This photograph from 1926 shows Alfred Spruce (left) and the foreman Jack Brace standing by the company's first motor van. The company's other transport was horse-drawn.

A postcard scene of the Model Laundry in the 1920s. The laundry is in a position between houses which today's planners would never allow.

Two form photographs of Oldswinford Junior School (dates unknown). The top photograph includes Iris Skelding, Joan Woodhouse, George Tandy, Leonard Fisher, Alan Webb and Geoff Noke. In the picture below are the Brown twins, ? King, Alan Webb, Joan Woodhouse, George Tandy, Geoff Noke, ? Leonard (or Leonora ?), ? Hollingsworth, Keith Yeadon, Frank Jewess.

The choir and church officials of Oldswinford Parish Church, 1928. Identified are Harold Heathcote, Billie Bridge, Richard Chance (churchwarden), Howard Farmer (former licensee of the Crown, Pedmore), Bill Niblett, Donald Lambert (organist and choirmaster), the Revd H.H. Williams, ? Hingley, ? Yardley, ? Nock, Bert Hill, Richard Hill, Alfred Cook, Harold Raybould, George Mason.

Pedmore Rectory in 1885 with three of the children of the Revd Mr W.A. Jones with either their mother or nanny.

The Oldswinford Home Guard Company. We are fortunate to have been able to identify many of what has become affectionately known as 'Dad's Army'. Back row, left to right: Joe Dunwell, Handel Pearsall, Tommy Norden, Dickie Norden, -?-, -?-, -?-, Chris Niblett, ? Heathcote, Alf Russell, -?-, Tom Franks, ? Clark, Horace Greenaway, -?-. Middle row: E. Roden, Lance Corporal Harry Wood,

Corporal Bill Powell, Sergeant Tommy Chance, (officer?) ? Scott, Jim Pearsall, Lance Corporal Ted Franks. Front row, extreme left, Johnny Shilvock, third from left Stan Roden and extreme right Arthur Cunningham.

In close-knit communities life has always seemed to revolve round the church and in the nineteenth century this was certainly the case in Wollaston where the Revd George Gilbanks was vicar from 1860 until his death on 4 January 1913, aged eighty-seven. In his fifty-three years ministry in Wollaston he had seen his parish grow from being a small, mainly agricultural, community into a thriving outpost of Stourbridge. When he died this 'In Memoriam' postcard was published. Mr Gilbanks was a native of Cumbria and came to Wollaston when he was thirty-four. He became involved in a number of organisations and played a major part in helping the poor of the parish as, at that time, there were no public welfare services. According to an obituary in the *County Express* Mr Gilbanks was also remembered for the close links he established between church and school.

This picture shows children outside the school with the early English style of church architecture seen to good effect, 1910.

This wedding photograph is of one of Mr Gilbanks's six children, his daughter Mabel, but we do not have the name of the groom or the date of the wedding. Mr and Mrs Gilbanks are on the bride's left. Also in the group are their son Ernest (back row, left) and daughters Lily (back row, fourth) and, next to her, Kate.

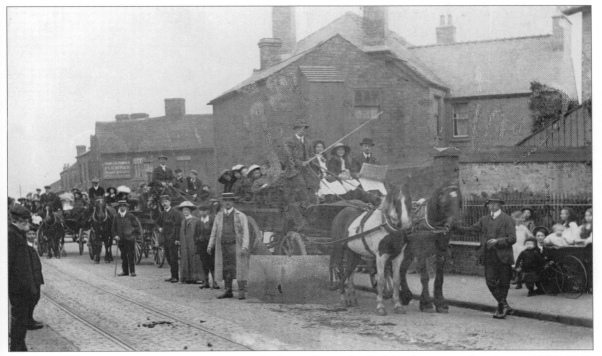

Pupils from Wollaston School prepare to set out by horse-drawn 'brakes' for their annual outing, *c.* 1900. Their destination is not stated although a popular venue for such events was Kinver, only 4 miles away.

Miss Gilbanks led the church's men's Bible class for many years and she is pictured here with the class in 1906. Only two others have been identified – the Bache brothers; Rupert (third from the left, middle row) and Aubrey (fifth from left also in the middle row). Aubrey Bache's family owned a spade and fork works on the corner of Mamble Road and Bowling Green Road. He was also at one time the licensee of the Queen's Head, Enville Street, later to become the Queensberry.

Identified here only as Wollaston Old Boys Football team of 1910/11, the club may have been formed by former pupils of the local school. Back row, left to right: Mr Arnold, H. Jenkins, M. Hall, H. Ellis, B. Jane, W. Baggott. Middle row: W. Thompson, W. Arnold, W. Eellett, F. Smith, F. Male. Front row:  C. Wall, N. Pagett, F. Heathcote.

A well-known family in Wollaston was the Harpers who ran a dairy business in Firgrove. In this 1938 photograph (above) haymaking is under way in the orchard. Pictured, left to right, are Jim Saunders, 'Dad' Harper, Hazel Porter, Frank Harper (on the cart), Jeff Tomlinson and Betty Porter. Below in a much earlier photograph is 'Grandad Harper' in his delivery cart.

After an injury while working as a chainmaker, Will Harris retrained as a butcher and started a business at the rear of the Alexandra Inn where he was licensee. Later he purchased the two cottages next door, converted one into a butcher's shop and used the other as his family home. This picture was taken in the early 1920s with Mr Harris in the shop doorway.

To work for over sixty years with one firm is almost unheard of nowadays. But that is precisely what Frank Male of Park Road West, Wollaston, did. He worked for Thomas Webb & Sons glassworks between 1907 and February 1968 and was seventy-four when he retired. He volunteered for the army in 1915 but served only two months with the Grenadier Guards. His former employers needed him for urgent war work and he returned to the glassworks – but officially remained in the Army until the war ended.

Wollaston carnival procession in High Street with the (unnamed) Carnival Queen and her attendants passing Firmstone Street in the 1930s. The cart was owned by A. & C. Cross.

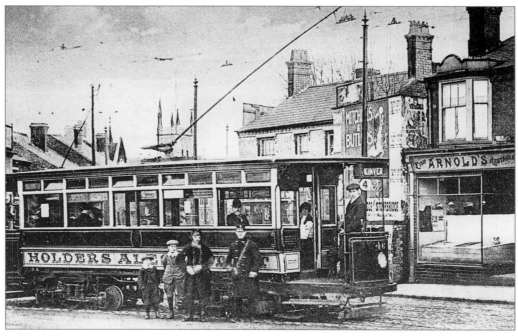

A scene some fifteen years earlier at Wollaston Junction featuring an Amblecote-bound tramcar (no. 40). This postcard scene was specially commissioned by a local confectioner and newsagent, Charles Smalley.

A picture of the oddly named N.W.B. Entire public house at the junction of Bridgnorth Road (Enville Street) and Mamble Road, 1896. Licensee William Henry Bowen is pictured with his wife Mary Ann, their youngest daughters Alice (in the pram), Jill and another daughter whose name is unrecorded. The pub was later renamed The Lion and, later still, The Stourbridge Lion.

The old Barley Mow which was demolished in more recent times to make way for a new pub. The group in the doorway is presumably the unnamed licensee and his family.

A rare pre-war aerial photograph of the borders of Amblecote and Stourbridge. At the top of the picture is Amblecote parish church, below which is Stourbridge gas works. To the left (centre) is the Jones & Attwood works. At the bottom the Stourbridge Canal interchange basin and wharves can be seen. Three narrowboats can just be spotted alongside the railway line, while to the left is the canal tunnel running under Stourbridge Road to the Bonded Warehouse (out of shot). The canal basin was filled in, the railway removed and the Mill Lane industrial estate was created after this time.

The Jones & Attwood Works Band which was in popular demand and a welcome sight at many public events in the area, *c.* 1920.

An early 1920s picture of Holloway End, Amblecote. The buildings to the left were once used as a boarding school established in 1853 by Philip Marks as 'Amblecote Training School in union with the Royal College Preceptors'. It closed in the 1890s, the two-storey building becoming the Royal Oak which, in turn, was replaced by a modern building. Amblecote Villa (right) still stands alongside the football and cricket ground car park.

Looking up Brettell Lane – a peaceful scene compared with today's traffic mayhem.

Mr G. Denton, a qualified herbalist, owned this shop in Holloway End and also plied his trade at various markets and tram stops to meet his customers. Mr Denton, a small man in build, is seen in the doorway with his wife. Because he was not very tall he was known locally as 'Denty the little pill mon'.

The junction of Collis Street (right), High Street and Wollaston Road (left), early 1900s. The time on the shop's clock is 8.45 a.m., and children are on their way to school. The shop has been replaced by a car dealership and garage forecourt. To the left is the Little Pig public house.

A rare picture of the centre of Amblecote presumably taken from the top of a glasscone in Wollaston Road, *c.* 1920. The tramcar is arriving at The Fish Inn (right) from Kinver and, judging by the queue of passengers waiting to board for Kinver, this could have been on a Saturday or Sunday. The road stretching into the distance is Collis Street while to the right of the pub on the corner is the entrance into the Kinver Light Railway tram depot.

Scouting had a strong following in Amblecote and this is the size of the parish church troop in 1936. The photograph was taken in the grounds of the old Vicarage. The vicar (pictured) at the time was Father Crabbe.

The Court of Honour – no explanation is given of its purpose – at the Amblecote Scout Camp at Westwood Park, near Droitwich, 1921. Pictured are Father H.M. Crabbe with, on his left, Stan Harper and Arthur Walker and on his right George Penn. The scouts standing and on the grass are unidentified.

Amblecote Cubs and Scouts assemble for the camera before their 1956 annual camp at Newquay, Wales. The lorry which carried the equipment was loaned by Edward Webb & Sons, Seed Merchants of Wordsley.

Corbett Hospital served the rapidly expanding areas of Stourbridge, Lye, Cradley Heath, Quarry Bank, Kingswinford and Wordsley for many years as a general hospital. As an accident and emergency unit it gained a reputation for efficiency. However, all that was to change and the hospital is now only a shadow of its former self, with emergency patients facing a long journey (usually through heavy traffic around the Merry Hill shopping centre) to reach Russells Hall Hospital, Dudley.

Some of the sisters and nurses at Corbett Hospital. Substantial amounts of money were raised by public subscription and events to finance the running of the hospital and one of the most popular events in the district was the hospital's carnival and fête. One of the carnival floats is seen here on 20 June 1931.

Two photographs of the Thomas Webb glassworkers. The above picture, dating from about 1914, was taken during a working day but sadly we have no names. Neither were there any names attached to the lower picture of Webb workers pictured in carefree mood at this works party, *c.* 1930.

These exotic costumes (particularly the one in the centre, made of wood shavings inviting people to 'chip in') were all part and parcel of those taking part in Stourbridge and district's fund-raising during the Corbett Hospital annual fête.

A 1920s photograph of the Little Pig Bowling Club, Amblecote. Seven of the members can be identified. They are: (back row fifth left) Charlie Rowberry and (seventh left) Sam Timmins. Middle row: (third left) Bert Jenkins, (fifth left) Syd Wilcox, (eighth left) David Mallen. Front row: Ted Nash, George Hughes and Jim Cope. Mr Cope's father founded H. Cope (funeral directors) of Cradley Heath and was a cabinet maker by trade.

The authors would be surprised if many people could instantly identify the location of this photograph. If the picture was taken today, the photographer would be standing on the traffic island near the Foley Arms, Pedmore. The house on the right is Pedmore Lodge and the road immediately to the right is Hagley Road. To the left is Ham Lane and ahead is Pedmore Lane. The small traffic island and its lamp-post were cleverly decorated to resemble a ship to commemorate the Coronation of King George V in 1911.

The final picture of our selection captures the atmosphere of a more gracious period – a wintry though peaceful scene of Oldswinford Castle from its grounds. The house was later converted to apartments and lost its particular architectural appeal.

# ACKNOWLEDGEMENTS

The authors gratefully acknowledge the help, advice and personal photographic collections provided by: Pat Burrage, Mr S. Eveson, Peter Greenslade, Richard Hargreaves, Bernard Hewins MBE, Mr J. Milner, Mr and Mrs Noke, Mr and Mrs Roden, Bernard Shaw, Robert Spruce, Brian Standish, Mrs Joan White and the Kidderminster Railway Museum. The authors also wish to acknowledge the wealth of information provided in *Stourbridge in Times Past* (Countryside Publications) by former local journalist and founder member and past-President of Stourbridge Historical and Archaeological Society, H. Jack Haden.